MW00640087

7 Keys for
Finding Jesus in the
Book of Revelation

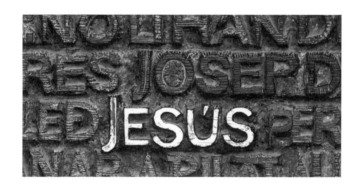

STEVE CASE & DANIEL WYSONG

Published by Involve Youth, P.O. Box 2424, Carmichael, CA 95609
Printed in the United States of America

Designed by Kari McKinney

The authors assume full responsibility for the accuracy of all
facts and quotations as cited in this book.

You can obtain additional copies of this book by visiting
www.Revelation101.com.

Case, Steve, 1957–
7 Keys for finding Jesus in the book of revelation,
by Steve Case and Daniel Wysong.

ISBN 13: 978-0-9850097-0-0 (paperback)
ISBN 10: 0-9850097-0-5 (paperback)

12 13 14 15 • 5 4 3 2 1

Dedicated to the hundreds of scholars who have spent thousands of hours/days/years to help others to discover the Revelation of Jesus Christ

Table of Contents

Chapter 1

Introduction

W e avoided the book of Revelation.
For years.
Perhaps you have, too.

Or maybe you're just the opposite. You might be the type who quickly darts to every mention of the word, like a hummingbird flitting from flower to flower in search of more nectar to keep those wings in constant motion.

Either way, this booklet could be the very thing you want and need.

How We Got Into This

Our avoidance of Revelation came from three main causes:

1. Burnout from heavy exposure to repeated emphasis on the latest news story or magazine cover article that surely could be interpreted as the end of the world (again).

2. Confusion when reading the book of Revelation ourselves. It seemed like the 2nd Coming of Christ happens several times during the book, and the flow of the book makes absolutely no sense. Maybe somebody took the book, put it in a blender, and then pasted the pieces together in hodgepodge fashion. Somebody needs to make sense of this concoction.

3. Frustration over the gridlock of the existing schools of interpretation for Revelation. Once you pick your school of interpretation, everything has to fit into that school, whether or not it really does fit. Dialogue between different schools seems difficult since they run in different currents. Furthermore, we had difficulty with some parts of the school with which we identified, but didn't find the other schools to be compelling.

So we stayed away from it.

And then, in a small group bible study one of us led, the group decided they wanted to study Revelation. After strongly avoiding it and coercing the group into picking a different book of the Bible, the gnawing question lingered, "Why am I resisting a study of the book of Revelation?" The reasons already stated came into focus.

Prodded by our friends and family, supported by a local church and conference, the two of us joined to form a team with accountability, a sounding board, and a positive response to "Let's study the book of Revelation." We began to take a fresh look at the familiar and intimidating final book in the Bible.

What we found with a renewed study both shocked and inspired us. We should make it plain at the outset that we are not Biblical scholars. We aren't new to Scripture. Both of us hold graduate degrees from the Seventh-day Adventist Theological Seminary at Andrews University. But we haven't spent decades pouring over ancient Greek and Hebrew texts, nor have we read hundreds of commentaries or directed doctoral students in focused research on Revelation. We are pastors. We spend time in the Word, with people, on church committees, preaching, teaching, praying, baptizing, marrying, burying, dedicating, counseling, planning, celebrating, evangelizing, listening, serving, visiting, organizing, remodeling, fund raising, etc.

We found ourselves drawn to several key scholars who have culled from many other scholars whose insights enthused us. ("Enthused" from the Greek *enthous* means "God within.") While these fine scholars shouldn't be blamed for our use or misuse of their work, we would be remiss not to mention them. They show amazing similarity in their work even though they have done much of their work independently of each other. The three that galvanized us are Dr. Jon Paulien, Dr. Ranko Stefanovic, and Dr. Jacques Doukhan.[1] They have built on the shoulders of other scholars who preceded them.[2] We give thanks to God for the work of these scholars and for their published findings. If we had been able to read their works earlier, perhaps we wouldn't have avoided the book of Revelation as long as we did.

As we studied, we found ourselves in territory new to us. It became helpful to check each other when the occasional far-fetched thought, thin connection, or unwarranted interpretation surfaced. The steps we took to understand Revelation coalesced into the seven keys presented in this booklet. Our local church, with conference support, sponsored a Revelation seminar for us to share with others what we had discovered. We presented the keys for finding Jesus in the book of Revelation, and then we went through the entire book as a group.

> "We found ourselves in territory new to us."

Our denomination has a history of lengthy Revelation seminars, sometimes running five nights a week for five or six weeks, yielding 25-30 presentations. Often these start with the book of Revelation and then springboard to various church doctrines. We reduced the number of presentations to 10 and chose to study Revelation rather than springboard to doctrines. We anticipated that doctrines reside in the book, but we made the study of the book our primary intention rather than a study of topics. We gathered together one night a week for 90 minutes per session.

When the studies concluded, we found that many of the participants were thrilled with the revelation of Jesus they had discovered, and then they wanted to know more about our Church and its beliefs. The pastors followed up the Revelation 101 series with a doctrinal Bible class. The church pastors began a series that covered those topics. We shouldn't have been surprised that the revelation of Jesus led to a desire for more study and affiliation.

A number of people asked for a set of the Revelation materials so they could do similar studies. What you hold in your hands is the introduction to that series, with just the seven keys for finding Jesus in the book of Revelation. According to Revelation 1:1, that's the purpose of the book—to reveal Jesus! The full series will go to press once we do the last edits after receiving final feedback from scholars, pastors, educators, and small group bible study leaders. We expect that will be available later in 2012 and accessible at the following website: www.Revelation101.com.

Getting Into the Book of Revelation

The book of Revelation begins by stating its intention: "The Revelation of Jesus Christ." While it is easy to read Revelation and start focusing on beasts and persecution, is this really what John intended for his readers when he wrote it? Is this what God intended when He gave it—a true revelation of Jesus Christ?

> The book of Revelation begins by stating its intention: "The Revelation of Jesus Christ."

At times it seems that Revelation serves as a magnet for those considered weird, anti-social, and paranoid. Perhaps that's why so many people simply avoid it. And yet Revelation 1:3 promises a blessing to those who read and hear the words of this prophecy. Have you experienced a blessing when you've read the book of Revelation? Would you like to be blessed by doing so?

What comes to mind when you think of the book of Revelation? Those who have studied this in the past will naturally draw on what they remember from their study. Many think of predicting the future, how the world will end, identifying who the bad guys are, trying to figure out exactly where we are on a timeline that leads to the very end! It is easy to get intensely into the book and later burn out when events don't transpire as expected and the end doesn't come.

It's natural for humans to try to find ourselves in the pages of Scripture. It's what we do when we look at a group photo: "Where am I?" (And why does the person standing next to me look better than I do?!) Unfortunately, this tendency can warp our view of Scripture, leading us to think the 144,000 is about me. (And why I'm just a bit more special than the other people who may go to heaven, but really aren't part of the 144,000.) This perspective conditions our brain to view the book of Revelation and the events leading up to the Second Coming from a very egocentric point of view: What *I* believe, the persecution that happens to *me*, where *I* will be, *my* righteous acts, the crown given to *me*... It's all about *me, Me, ME!!!*

That's why the overall purpose of Revelation needs to receive repeated emphasis. Otherwise it's easy to slip into misleading trails, obscure details, and a focus on us rather than on Jesus. But the litmus test of any study of Revelation is whether or not Jesus gets revealed.

We want more of a revelation of Jesus Christ, don't you?

Chapter 2

Schools of Interpretation

Most people who begin a study of Revelation already have a certain framework in mind as they read. This colors and influences them as they interpret the messages in the Bible. And some Bibles have study guides in the margins or at the bottom of each page to assist in the interpretation of this highly symbolic book, further reinforcing presuppositions about the text.

Are you aware of which school of interpretation you follow? It's easy to say, "I follow the Bible," but each one of these schools of interpretation follows the Bible. So the question becomes, "*How* do you follow the Bible?" We have found that the majority of the people we interact with regarding the book of Revelation know of only two schools of interpretation: 1) My school (the correct one); and 2) anyone who thinks differently (the wrong one).

The various understandings of the book of Revelation can be placed into four basic schools of interpretation. Depending on which school of interpretation you follow, your interpretation of Revelation will become fairly predictable![1] Let's take a brief overview of these four schools and the likely interpretations that come from each one.

1. The Past (officially called "Preterist" which comes from the Latin word *praeteritus* which means the past, literally "what came before") This first school sees Revelation as a history of the first century AD. John's letter to the seven churches served to encourage them in a difficult time of persecution from the Roman powers. The "bad guys" are the Roman Empire and also Jews who persecuted the Christians. Of course the "good guys" are Christians. Calamity could refer to the fall of Jerusalem in AD 70 or future persecution that would take place shortly after the book was written. This school of interpretation has little relevance for us today since it wasn't written for us. However, we can see what God did in the past. Most mainline Protestants and Catholics follow this school.

2. The Future (officially called the "Futurist" school of interpretation) Following the description of the seven churches that ends with Revelation 3, this school believes rest of the book describes in symbolic form what will take place in the future. The starting point for all of this is a secret rapture in which Jesus snatches his faithful followers to heaven and those left on earth begin a seven-year period until Jesus visibly returns. Some variations of this have the seven-years as a time of tribulation (or "time of trouble"), while others divide the seven years in half and have tribulation for only part of this time. This dispensation theology has become common doctrine for many evangelicals in the past 100 years. But because it's all in the future, various interpretations abound. The test of time is yet in the future, so who knows who has it right? Often the latest news or natural disaster ignites a fresh possibility for the futurists, but then it dies out or a newer version takes center stage.

Hal Lindsay's *Late Great Planet Earth* in the 1970s popularized this view. More recently, the *Left Behind* series of novels by Tim LaHaye and Jerry Jenkins tapped into this school of interpretation. Just about anyone or anything can be the projected bad guys of the future. For Americans, Communism was the major threat (think of the Soviet Union or Eastern European countries). More recently, China, India or Arab countries could be named as potential "bad guys" from an American perspective. The Muslim world seems more of a threat today than 50 years ago. Not surprisingly, people from other countries would label the United States as the "bad guy." The economy sometimes gets pegged as the catalyst that will bring about the end. Natural disasters such as earthquakes, floods, hurricanes, fires, or drought could trigger a new, end time scenario, with a vacuum for control that the bad guys capitalize on for our destruction. You could probably come up with several examples from the past 12 months. Because of the sensational nature of the futurist school, it creates quite a stir whenever a new event or explanation grabs the headlines, but it usually doesn't last. Do you find yourself excited by the latest news or does it make you skeptical? This will influence how you read the book of Revelation.

3. History (officially called the "Historicist" school of interpretation) This school believes Revelation covers the span of history from the early Christian Church until Christ's second coming. The book of Revelation describes what occurs over that time period in the great conflict between good and evil—between Christ and Satan. Different countries, kingdoms, wars, and other events come into view and have been predicted in Revelation's prophecies. Interpreters simply need to study history (primarily the history of Western Civilization) and one can plug into the various symbols presented in Revelation. Sometimes these connections are obvious, and at other times it takes ingenuity or creativity or finding an obscure bit of history in order to make the connections.

> Can you identify which school of interpretation seems like the right one to you?

Martin Luther and a number of other Reformers followed this school of interpretation. The bad guys were the dominant powers that negatively impacted the reformers, which was primarily the Catholic Church. (Not surprisingly, the Catholic Church's response was an emphasis on the two earlier schools of interpretation already mentioned, the past and the future, which they needed in order to take some heat off of themselves in that present time!) The good guys are the true Christians, not the Christians-in-name-only or the Christians who have been part of the existing, old system. History will show how God's people have repeatedly fallen short of what God wanted. The best hope is a few good people, a remnant, at the end of history that God will rescue from this evil world, through the "narrow gate," and take to heaven to be with him. This is the school of interpretation the Seventh-day Adventist Church has followed. If you have a Seventh-day Adventist background, this might be the only school of interpretation you've known. Also, if you have a strong bias against the Catholic Church or the Christian Church throughout history, this would be a good interpretation to utilize. Today, very few denominations adhere to the history school of interpretation even though it still remains one of the established schools of interpretation.

4. **Spiritual** (sometimes called the "Symbolic" or "Idealist" school of interpretation) In contrast to labeling any religious or political institution as "the bad guys," the idealist school of interpretation follows a much more personal application of the book of Revelation. Symbols are helpful in making specific applications from one individual to another. And fresh applications can be made over time, repeatedly. Everyone faces tough times, and God seeks to reach each person where they are. When a person reads the book of Revelation, this will become clear in some areas, while other areas might not apply to that given individual, or at least not until later. Each person is free to find one's own meaning in the book of Revelation. "What does this mean to you right now?" functions as the most important question.

In describing these four basic schools of interpretation, our hope is simply to provide a description of each, not to evaluate the one that is right and which ones are wrong. Can you identify which school of interpretation, at least initially, seems like the right one to you? If you're more visual than verbal, consider Figure 1.

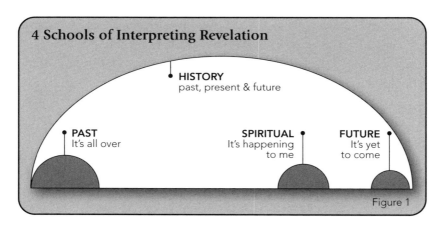

Figure 1

Let's try out these four schools of interpretation on one short segment in Revelation to see how we can get four fairly different interpretations when we read the very same verses out of the Bible. Consider the opening of the first of seven seals.

Revelation 6:1-2[2] reads, "I watched as the Lamb opened the first of the seven seals. Then I heard one of the four living creatures say in a voice like thunder, 'Come!' (*verse 2*) I looked, and there before me was a white horse! Its rider held a bow, and he was given a crown, and he rode out as a conqueror bent on conquest."

Notice how each school of interpretation has its own way of explaining the first seal:

1. Past – The white horse symbolizes the Roman leader, Titus, who is bringing judgment on the apostate city, Jerusalem, that killed the prophets and then the Messiah. He will conquer Jerusalem as part of God's vengeance against evil.

2. Future – A white horse would be considered to be good. Don't be fooled! This isn't Christ, but the Antichrist, going out to conquer the earth. This happens after God's people have been secretly raptured to heaven. This Antichrist is the same as the terrible sea beast of Revelation 13.

3. History – a white horse symbolizes what is good. The bow indicates the rider is armed, going out on conquest. This first seal symbolizes the initial surge of taking the Gospel to the world in the first century AD. Additional seals will cover later periods of history.

4. Spiritual – God rides victoriously. Whoever rules as a king or national leader does so only because God has placed that person there, and God can take that same person down—as evidenced throughout the course of history. God is in control.

Each school of interpretation is following the Bible, but each school has its own rules, which results in very different interpretations of the same verses in Scripture.

What should a person do? It's no wonder that there is so much confusion and disagreement over what the book of Revelation actually reveals.

For our study, we will intentionally *not* follow one particular school of interpretation! Instead, we will take a different approach to the book. Some may consider this a completely new way to study the book of Revelation, but we think it's actually the oldest way there is. Bible scholars would describe it as an exegetical approach. You may be familiar with the idea of reading the Bible "in context." We'll just call it "Bible Explanation."

Most of us have a natural tendency to see in the Bible what we want to see, not necessarily want the Bible says. If we come to the text with presuppositions, we are in great danger of manipulating the Bible to fit a certain way of thinking we've already determined. As the authors, we admit that our background is the History school, so we may have long-term leanings that direction. But our desire is to "let the text change us," instead of "us changing the text."

> It's no wonder that there is so much confusion and disagreement.

As we seek to take an unbiased view of Revelation, sometimes we'll come up with the same interpretation as the Past. And sometimes it will be more like the Future. Some will match the History school and still others will sound more like the Spiritual school of interpretation. We're not trying to match up with any one of those schools. Our attempt with the Bible Explanation approach is to find the interpretation within the Bible itself.

We'll still have several rules or guidelines to help us. We'll call them "keys" for finding Jesus in the book of Revelation. We won't just look at a verse really intently and then see what creative explanation our brains might conjure up for consideration. We'll actually utilize seven keys or guidelines for the Bible Explanation approach. They will be the next seven chapters of this booklet. The first four are what you are likely to use when you study any book of the Bible, and you are probably already familiar with them. These don't change with the book of Revelation. The last three keys that complete the seven keys are unique to the last book of the Bible, because it is indeed such an unusual book! Unless you've studied the book of Revelation in some depth, these last three keys might have some surprising elements in them. If you've studied Revelation in the past, these will probably resonate with you.

In addition to explaining each key, we will illustrate each one with some examples from the book of Revelation. We'll use primarily examples from the first part of the book as a starting point. The reader can then use these same keys to continue through the rest of the book. A verbatim of presentations for utilizing these seven keys for the entire book of Revelation will be available at www.Revelation101.com in 2012. For right now, it's time to begin the seven keys for finding Jesus in the book of Revelation.

Chapter 3

Key #1: Literary Context

Those with a high regard for the Bible sometimes take a verse or phrase from Scripture and make a direct application to someone's life today. Quoting 2 Timothy 3:16-17 (NKJV) they recite, "All Scripture is given by inspiration of God, and is profitable for doctrine, for reproof, for correction, for instruction in righteousness, that the man of God may be complete, thoroughly equipped for every good work."

That can set the stage for helpful messages from God or for toxic manipulations. For example, a potentially helpful message would be 1 Samuel 16:7, which reads, "The Lord does not look at the things human beings look at. People look at the outward appearance, but the Lord looks at the heart." Most of us have a tendency to make quick judgments based on what we see on the outside of a person. But God doesn't get distracted by that. He looks at what a person is like on the inside—one's heart and character.

An example of a toxic manipulation could be using 1 Chronicles 21:7 (NLT), which says, "God was very displeased with the census, and he punished Israel for it." Americans could take this isolated verse and declare that God doesn't want America to even take a census or else America will suffer God's punishment! The final punctuation could come in a statement such as, "I'm not saying that, the Bible says it!"

Indeed, the Bible should be applied to our personal lives, but simply ripping a phrase from Holy Writ doesn't guarantee that God's message matches what a person claims it says. How can we know?

The first key for finding Jesus in the book of Revelation is the literary context. In fact, this is the first key for understanding any part of the Bible. Sometimes people refer to this as "context" or "reading the Bible in context." This means you consider the verses before the verse you're studying, as well as the verses after it. You'll want to look at the context of an entire chapter or maybe the entire book.

A silly example of *not* following this first key is stringing a few verses together by taking them *out of context*. For example, we read in the Bible that "He [Judas]…went and hanged himself." (Matthew 27:5, NKJV) And then we can quote Jesus who said, "Go and do likewise." (Luke 10:27, NKJV) Staying with the words of Jesus, "What you do, do quickly." (John 13:27, NKJV) By taking these verses out of context and stringing them together, it sounds as though the Bible presents Jesus as a person who encourages us to go commit suicide, and to do it right away!

Bible studies that link a variety of verses from different parts of the Bible may show a theme throughout Scripture, or they may be unrelated and manipulated texts, ripped out of context, and used to say something they really don't mean.

Considering the literary context can prevent us from claiming the Bible says something that it doesn't actually say, and it also helps us to understand what the Bible really is saying.

Here's another example. Many Christians are familiar with the verse, "Behold I stand at the door and knock. If anyone hears my voice and opens the door, I will come in to him and dine with him, and he with me." (NKJV) Do you know which Gospel contains that verse—Matthew, Mark, Luke or John? Actually, it's not found in any of the Gospels. You'll find it in the book of Revelation, chapter three and verse 20.

Perhaps this verse has significant meaning to you. Maybe it was the verse that led to your decision to accept Christ into your life. If so, HALLELUJAH! But this verse is not about individuals accepting Christ, at least not in its context. (If you want that message in its context, try John 10:9-10, or John 10:27-28.)

Revelation 3:20, in its context, is not addressed to individuals, but to an entire church—the church of Laodicea. Revelation chapters two and three contain messages to seven different churches. The last one, Laodicea, can be found in Revelation 3:14-22. If you're familiar with this passage you know it's far from a "feel-good" message. This is the one in which Christ offers a rebuke for being lukewarm instead of being hot or cold. He even talks about vomiting this church out of his mouth. In fact, there isn't even one redeeming quality about this church. The verse immediately before it reads, "As many as I love, I rebuke and chasten. Therefore be zealous and repent." (Revelation 3:19, NKJV) Then

> What the Bible actually means might be different than what we've heard previously.

we have that familiar verse, "Behold I stand at the door and knock. If anyone hears my voice and opens the door, I will come in to him and dine with him, and he with me." (Revelation 3:20, NKJV)

This message is for an entire church, not simply an individual! Try to imagine Christ standing outside of an entire church, asking to come in. It sounds absolutely preposterous! Aren't the people in the church gathered to worship Christ? But he has been locked out! Is that even possible? Apparently it was. One wonders if the same thing could happen today.

Considering the literary context provides insight regarding what the Bible actually means, which might be different than what we've heard or taken to heart previously.

A unique element that would fall into key #1: the literary context, is what Revelation scholar Jon Paulien terms "duodirectionality."[1] Occasionally a verse in Revelation will summarize what precedes that verse and also provide a clue about what follows.

One verse looks two directions; hence the word "duodirectional." Here are three examples of it.

Revelation 6:17, "For the great day of their wrath has come, and who can withstand it?" The verses preceding this describe the sixth seal, including the "wrath of the Lamb" and the one sitting on the throne in heaven (God the Father). You can also read about the earth falling apart in Revelation 6:12-16. The description sounds so overwhelming that it begs the question John asks in verse 17, "Who can withstand it?" That's looking back.

> Duodirectional—
> it summarizes
> the verses
> preceding it and
> introduces
> the verses
> that follow.

Looking the other direction, the sixth chapter ends and all of chapter 7 describes the 144,000 and the great multitude. These are the ones who are able to withstand the wrath of the Lamb! Revelation 6:17 is duodirectional— it summarizes the verses preceding it and introduces the verses that follow.

Revelation 3:21 looks both directions. It reads, "To those who are victorious, I will give the right to sit with me on my throne, just as I was victorious and sat down with my Father on his throne." The previous two chapters described seven churches and each church received a message for the "victorious." This particular verse applies first of all to the seventh church, Laodicea, found in verses 14-22. But it also summarizes all seven churches. And it introduces the concept of sitting with Christ on his throne. That topic receives a more detailed treatment in Revelation chapters four and five. So Revelation 3:21 summarizes the previous two chapters and introduces the next two chapters. It is duodirectional.

Another duodirectional verse in Revelation carries special significance because it introduces the second half of the book. You can find it in Revelation 11:18. It reads, "The nations were angry, and your wrath has come. The time has come for judging the dead, and for rewarding your servants the prophets and your people who revere your name, both great and small—and for destroying those who destroy the earth."

That one verse packs a lot into those comparatively few words. It summarizes the seven trumpets of Revelation chapters eight through eleven. But it also provides an outline for Revelation chapters 12-22!

"The nations were angry" introduces chapters 12-14.

"Your wrath has come" gives an overview of chapters 15-18.

"The time to judge the dead" previews chapters 19-20.

"Rewarding your people" gives a snapshot of chapters 21-22.

It might take a Revelation scholar to point out something like this to us, but once we see it, new perspectives immediately come to our attention. We're left with a certain sense of awe that God has already sent these messages to us and we simply needed to pause, study, and perceive what's already in the Bible. The literary context matters!

Our first key to find Jesus in the book of Revelation is the literary context. What does the Bible say, in context? Be sure to check it out, not just a verse or phrase in isolation. Check the literary context!

Chapter 4

Key #2: Historical/Cultural Context

The second key for finding Jesus in the book of Revelation is the historical context. Some refer to this as the cultural context. Many things that just seem "normal" or things we often take for granted color the way we view a message. In order to understand a message in its historical context, we need to understand the history and culture when it was written. This might be very different from our history and culture. This is true when comparing different eras of history or different cultures even at the same point in history.

With a book like the Bible, written over a span of more than 1,500 years, you would expect some similarities and some differences based on the historical context. For example, the historical context of Egyptian slavery for God's people was quite different from when David and Solomon ruled the kingdom during Israel's "Golden Age."

Because John wrote the book of Revelation nearly 2,000 years ago, we would expect a number of things to be different. As a result, we will need to understand the historical context in order to better understand the message of Revelation.

A look at the messages to the seven churches becomes much more pointed and practical when considering the historical context for each one. Sometimes a message to one church is similar to the message to another church, and sometimes it can be very different. But the person reading needs to understand the historical context of that particular church in order to understand the meaning of the message written to that church. Otherwise the reader will probably start with what the message means to that particular reader today and then project that onto the church back then. That's the opposite of understanding what it meant to that church and then applying that meaning to our day.

You don't need a span of 2,000 years to find something to be distinctly different. For example, in Romans 13:1-7, Paul wrote that followers of God should be subject to the governing authorities, because God placed them there for our good. Paul wrote this less than 40 years before John wrote the book of Revelation, yet John makes some pretty strong hints about *not* following the governing authorities (see Rev. 6:4; 7:14; 11:7-13; 12:17, etc.) Does this mean the Bible contradicts itself? It certainly seems like that unless you understand the historical context.

When Paul wrote to the Romans that the government had been set in place by God and they should follow it, he was probably ministering in the town of Corinth, a place where he received the benefits of the Roman government in contrast to the Jewish persecution that often came his way.

But by the time John wrote the book of Revelation, the Roman government had begun to torture and kill Christians. Let's not forget that John, the pastor in Ephesus, did not write the book of Revelation from his church office in Ephesus. According to Revelation 1:9 (NKJV), "I, John, both your brother and companion in the tribulation and kingdom and patience of Jesus Christ, was on the island that is called Patmos for the word of God and for the testimony of Jesus Christ."

Here's John's message when one includes some historical context: Pastor John had been through some tough times from the Romans, who had banished him to a deserted island. John is a prisoner of Rome because he's a follower of Jesus. Based on that history, which is quite different from Paul's experience when he wrote the book of Romans, we can begin to understand how two inspired writers wrote such different things.

Another example of the historical context providing insight into the Bible can be seen simply by reading what is in the text. We read the book of Revelation because we believe it was written for us. But you can find the initial audience right in the first chapter. Look at Revelation 1:4, "John, to the seven churches in the province of Asia." In case that isn't obvious enough, skip ahead to verse 11, "Write on a scroll what you see and send it to the seven churches, to Ephesus, Smyrna, Pergamum, Thyatira, Sardis, Philadelphia, and Laodicea."

There are a number of elements written specifically to these seven churches that have application for us today as well. But it is also important to keep in mind what is actually written in the text—the initial target group for the book of Revelation is the seven churches in what is now Turkey.

What difference does this make? Well, some people imagine that John was somewhat unaware of what God was doing to him and through him as he wrote the book of Revelation. Their frame of reference is so centered on their current life that they figure John saw our day and didn't know how to describe it, especially with our technology and other elements that he wouldn't be able to understand. So maybe he used symbols because he couldn't explain helicopters or computers or nuclear holocaust. But by looking at the historical/cultural context, we

> The book of Revelation had immediate implications in the first century AD.

see that the book of Revelation had immediate implications in the first century AD. That's why John addressed it to those seven churches. And because it's a supernatural book, it continues to speak to us today.

Sometimes a basic understanding of the historical context simply provides deeper understanding and appreciation of the message in the Bible—a message that we can then apply to our current situation. For example, in Revelation 1:18 we read, "I am the Living One. I was dead, and now look, I am alive for ever and ever! And I hold the keys of death and Hades." The message seems rather straight-forward: Jesus is alive! He was dead, but he's not anymore. AND he has power over death, too!

That's correct. But the historical context adds even greater punch to it. Here's how: Have you ever heard of the cult of Hekate? When John wrote the book of Revelation, Hekate was a popular goddess in the area of the seven churches. People at that time believed Hekate traveled between heaven and earth, letting those on earth know what was happening in heaven, and letting those in heaven know what was happening on earth. What added to her "popularity" and importance was that she was the source of life and she held the keys to heaven and to Hades—she determined when you would die and where you would go after you died. No wonder she was so important.

With that little bit of historical background, now read Revelation 1:18, "I am the Living One. I was dead, and now look, I am alive for ever and ever! And I hold the keys of death and Hades." The message is still about Jesus. But with this historical/cultural context we see that John's message is a direct affront and challenge to the existing belief system and accepted worship of the time. John presents Jesus as the One with the keys. If Jesus holds the keys, then Hekate doesn't. So without ever naming Hekate, John's message is that Jesus trumps Hekate. Would you trust Jesus to replace any of the things that dominate our world today the way that Hekate did in John's day? The historical context reveals that the answer continues to be: "Definitely!"

How can a person find the historical/cultural context, especially those elements that are not included in the Bible? Scholars spend much of their time searching for and reading ancient documents. What they discover gets published in scholarly journals and then books. Some of these become textbooks for Bible students. Study Bibles often contain this type of material, even if stated briefly. Bible commentaries present more. The internet gives immediate access to scholarly findings as well as those that aren't very scholarly or accurate. Just Googling a topic doesn't guarantee anything accurate in the first 10 or even 100 responses. Anybody can set up a website and post something. Sources need to be verified, not merely stated on the internet.

Understanding the historical/cultural context can provide clarity and depth to the words of Scripture. Sometimes the historical context makes little difference to our understanding, and at other times it makes all the difference in the world!

Chapter 5

Key #3: Key Words

Just as the historical/cultural context sometimes make a big difference and sometimes it doesn't, the actual words within a text of Scripture sometimes are pregnant with meaning and at other times are just basic words. So the reader of Revelation will want to be on the lookout for the key words—the ones packed with extra insights and meaning. Sometimes these are obvious, and sometimes they aren't. Here are two examples from the very first verse of Revelation—Revelation 1:1 (NIV).

"The revelation of Jesus Christ, which God gave him to show his servants what must soon take place. He made it known by sending his angel to his servant John."

Several words jump out as potential key words. Consider the name of the book—Revelation! What comes to mind when you hear that word? Some think of beasts and symbols and destruction and mighty angels.

But what does the word itself mean? Well, the root word is *apocalypsis*, which means "to reveal." This word is the one you would use if something is cooking on the stove or over a fire and you came by and asked, "What's cooking?" Sometimes the smell will let you know; but sometimes you won't know until you take off the lid and then you receive a *revelation* of what's in the pot. Taking off the lid reveals what's inside.

Another way to illustrate what this one word "revelation" means is by considering what happens when a painting has been covered and that covering is about to be dropped. This will reveal a new piece of art to those who are looking.

This can be made personal. Do you already have a picture of Jesus Christ in your mind? The early Christians certainly did. By this time, very few who were Christians had actually ever seen Christ in person. They had heard about him. Others told them second and third hand how he had done many marvelous things, including miracles. They had heard of his teachings. Many times they remembered that he had been crucified on a cross, and his followers claimed he had been resurrected, and then taken to heaven. And they repeated the promise that one day soon Jesus would return to take them to heaven.

Does that match your picture of Jesus? Would you like to know more? Would you like a fresh revelation of Jesus Christ? Would you feel blessed when you receive that? John certainly revealed more about Jesus that the early Christians didn't know. And you can discover revelations of Jesus that you would never have if it weren't for this particular book of the Bible!

But the one word "revelation" needs to be seen in contrast with another word in Revelation 1:1. Most translations have masked this other key word so that the verse reads more smoothly. Here is Revelation 1:1 again from the New International Version: "The revelation of Jesus Christ, which God gave him to show his servants what must soon take place. He made it known by sending his angel to his servant John." Note the beginning of that second sentence. The NIV reads, "He made it known." Other translations have:

"He sent and communicated it" NASB
"So that John could share the revelation" NLT
"To show his servants" NCV, RSV, TEV, NKJV
"To make plain to his servants" MSG

As mentioned earlier, in order to smooth out this verse, most translations have missed the significance of a key word in Revelation 1:1. The old King James Version gets it right on this one! "The revelation of Jesus Christ, which God gave unto him, to shew unto his servants things which must shortly come to pass, and he sent and signified it by his angel unto his servant John."

Did you catch that unusual phrase? "He sent and *signified* it by his angel unto his servant John." That is a bit awkward. No wonder recent translations have smoothed it out. But what does it mean to signify something? For those into Greek words, the word John used was *semaino*, if that helps at all! It means to show by a sign or symbol. In other words, God symbolized his message to John!

That probably comes as no surprise to anyone who has read the book of Revelation. Can you find any symbols in the book? Of course you can! In fact, the book of Revelation is loaded with symbols. But by the words he selected in the

> Why didn't John just tell it like it is?

very first verse of this book John gives the reader and listeners a code to understand the entire book. In Revelation 1:1 John tells the readers that he is going to reveal Jesus to them in symbols. Those who expect a lot of literal images in the book need to pay special attention to the first verse—a revelation of Jesus Christ in symbolic format!

Some naturally wonder why John didn't just tell it like it is! Why did he use symbols? Didn't he realize that those reading it 2,000 years later might not understand those symbols, or maybe they would confidently say they know exactly what John meant even though they might actually misunderstand the symbols he used? Why did John reveal Jesus in this confusing manner of using symbols?

The historical context provides a hint. Christian Pastor John, in the city of Ephesus, had made things clear and plain regarding Jesus. This put him in conflict with the ruling power at the time—the Roman Empire. That's why he found himself on Patmos as a prisoner (see Revelation 1:9). While exiled, God gave

John visions with symbols to reveal Jesus to John's parishioners. We don't know what it took for John to get a message from the island of Patmos back to the mainland. It's likely that any message from a prisoner would be read and censored before it could leave Patmos. How could John send his message about Jesus, which certainly was in conflict with the Roman Empire, and yet get clearance from the Romans? By putting the message in code or symbols—that's how!

Where did John come up with the symbols he chose? Actually, the verse tells us: God gave it to John and sent it by an angel or messenger. So the symbols came from God. Perhaps the question that really needs an answer is, "How can we find out what these various symbols mean?" To put it another way, "How do we break the code?" Would you like to know? One of the keys will explain the code. Specifically, it will be key # 5.

But before we get to that unique key, there is one more key that is useful for understanding any passage of Scripture. We turn to that key now.

Chapter 6

Key #4: Compare with the Rest of Scripture

One evidence that the Bible is the inspired Word of God is the way 66 different books of the Bible blend together. Written by some 40 different authors over a span of more than 1,500 years, it continues to be relevant and life-changing: the Word of God!

A student of Scripture will find similarities when comparing one part of the Bible with another part. Sometimes one verse or passage will illuminate another one. For example, the Trinity (God the Father, God the Son, and God the Holy Spirit) can be found right in Revelation 1, although they aren't identified by those terms. Revelation 1:4-5 reads, "John, to the seven churches which are in Asia: Grace to you and peace from Him who is and who was and who is to come, and from the seven Spirits who are before His throne, and from Jesus Christ, the faithful witness, the firstborn from the dead, and the ruler over the kings of the earth."

The word "Trinity" doesn't appear, and the three members of the Trinity aren't named. But by making comparisons with the rest of Scripture, one can identify the Trinity in these opening verses of Revelation.

The most obvious gets named, "Jesus Christ." In case anyone wonders who that could be, he's "the firstborn from the dead." But to figure out the rest, you need to consider other portions of the Bible.

What about "Him who is and who was and who is to come"—
who is that? Before labeling this as another description of Jesus,
think back to when God called Moses at the burning bush (see
Exodus 3:14). God named himself as "I AM" or "I am that I am"
or "I am the one who is always in the present tense." That's another way of saying "Him who is and who was and who is to
come." This is Yahweh. We can refer to him as "God the Father."

Have you ever heard of "the seven Spirits who are before His
throne"? Revelation chapters two and three contain messages to
seven churches, and each is told to listen to what the Spirit says
to the churches. Revelation 4:5 describes seven lamps blazing before the throne and these are the seven spirits of God. In Revelation 5:6 one can read about a Lamb before the throne, and it has
seven horns and seven eyes, which get labeled as the seven Spirits
of God sent out into all the earth.

This same author, John, already wrote about Christ's message
to his disciples shortly before his crucifixion. Jesus explained
that although He would soon be leaving to return to heaven, he
promised to send the Holy Spirit to the disciples (see John 14).

The Old Testament has a reference for the seven Spirits. Isaiah
11:2 mentions seven different spirits: the spirit of the Lord, wis-
dom, understanding, counsel, might, knowledge, and fear of the
Lord. And Zechariah 4:1-6 describes seven gold lampstands with
seven channels feeding it. This is the familiar passage that includes,
"Not by might, nor by power, but by my Spirit says the Lord."

Just because we find a word or phrase in another place in the
Bible doesn't automatically demonstrate that it's the same thing.
But it's worth checking into and it sometimes provides much illu-
mination, which can be especially helpful in a book full of symbolic messages.

Here's one more example, taken from Revelation 1:13-16. This
passage describes an unusual person. Listen to these character-
istics, "Among the lampstands was someone like a Son of Man,
dressed in a robe reaching down to his feet and with a golden
sash around his chest. The hair on his head was white like wool,

as white as snow, and his eyes were like blazing fire. His feet were like bronze glowing in a furnace, and his voice was like the sound of rushing waters. In his right hand he held seven stars, and coming out of his mouth was a sharp, double-edged sword. His face was like the sun shining in all its brilliance."

Do you know anyone who matches this description? If you saw someone or something that looked like this, how would you describe it? Daniel 10:5-6 contains a similar description. You won't find a word-for-word copy, but compare this description with the one just mentioned in Revelation. Daniel 10:5-6 reads, "I looked up and there before me was a man dressed in linen, with a belt of fine gold from Uphaz around his waist. His body was like topaz, his face like lightning, his eyes like flaming torches, his arms and legs like the gleam of burnished bronze, and his voice like the sound of a multitude." The rest of the chapter makes it clear that Daniel has encountered a supernatural being.

> ## Did John see the same person that Daniel had seen 700 years before?

Did John, on the island of Patmos, see the same person in his vision that Daniel had seen 700 years before in Babylon?

Revelation draws from several portions of the book of Daniel, so comparing passages in Revelation with other portions of Scripture can yield tremendous results. It's not limited to just the book of Daniel. Our next key will show why. But the fourth key for finding Jesus in the book of Revelation is to compare with other passages of Scripture.

This concludes the first four keys. These keys can and should be used when studying all parts of the Bible, not just the book of Revelation. If you have some experience in studying Scripture, you probably already follow these keys. The next three keys are unique and important for studying the book of Revelation.

Chapter 7

Key #5: Old Testament Roots

If you've read different parts of the New Testament, you've probably come across various quotations from the Old Testament. For example, in the book of Matthew it almost seems like the writer goes out of his way to quote all kinds of Old Testament references. In Matthew 1:22, an angel explained to Joseph that Mary conceived her baby by means of the Holy Spirit. Then the Scriptures say, "All this took place to fulfill what the Lord had said through the prophet, 'The virgin will conceive and give birth to a son, and they will call him Immanuel.'" Your Bible might even have a footnote that indicates this quotation comes from Isaiah 7:14.

If you continue in Matthew chapter two, you'll come across additional references back to the Old Testament prophets. You might have to check the footnotes again to find the specific references for Micah and Hosea, but Jeremiah gets named right in the text in Matthew 2:17.

Jesus himself quoted the Old Testament. In Luke 4 Jesus responded to the devil's temptations by quoting from Deuteronomy. And when he went to the synagogue, Jesus read from Isaiah and then told the listeners that he was the fulfillment of the passage he read. When Jesus cleansed the temple shortly before his crucifixion, the religious leaders told him to silence the praising children. Jesus responded in Matthew 21:16, "Have you never read, 'From the lips of children and infants you have ordained praise'?" Jesus was quoting Psalm 8:2. No wonder Jesus told the crowd during the Sermon on the Mount, "Do not think I came to destroy the law or the prophets. I did not come to destroy but to fulfill them." Matthew 5:17 (NKJV)

We can find Old Testament references in other portions of the New Testament besides the Gospels. Paul's famous statement, "The just shall live by faith" found in Romans 2:17 is actually a quotation from Habakkuk 2:4. And in Romans 3:10 Paul explains that both Jews and Gentiles are guilty before God and in need of God's gift of salvation. When Paul says, "There is none righteous, no, not one; there is none who understands; There is none who seeks after God," he is not making this up. He's quoting from Psalm 14, and it's also found in Psalm 53.

Those who count the number of Old Testament quotations in the New Testament typically come up with about 300 examples. But when you consider allusions to the Old Testament, not exact quotations but there seems to be a connection to certain Old Testament portions of Scripture, the numbers climb into the thousands.

What about the book of Revelation? How many Old Testament references can be found there? If there are 300 references in the 27 books of the New Testament, how many are in Revelation? Ten or 20 or 50-100? This might come as a surprise, but there are no Old Testament quotations in the entire book of Revelation. That's right, zero; nada.

Here is a double challenge. The first challenge is to find any Old Testament quotation anywhere in the book of Revelation. The second challenge is to find as many Old Testament allusions or echoes—something that has its roots in the Old Testament—as you can in the book of Revelation. You won't find any direct quotations, but you'll find loads of Old Testament roots.

In our study or Revelation, we relied heavily of several Bible scholars, namely Jon Paulien, Ranko Stefanovic, and Jacques

Doukhan. These scholars have relied on others who have studied before they did. Dr. Paulien and Dr. Stefanovic are New Testament scholars. Dr. Doukhan is an Old Testament scholar. Some wonder why we would draw from an Old Testament scholar. Well, Dr. Doukhan actually wrote a commentary on the book of Revelation. That's right, an Old Testament scholar wrote a commentary on a New Testament book. But why? Dr. Doukhan claims there are more than 2,000 Old Testament roots in the book of Revelation! That's right, more than 2,000!

That raises the question, Can we really understand the book of Revelation if we *don't* have a foundational understanding of the Old Testament? Without the Old Testament, interpreting the book of Revelation is like touring the Grand Canyon in a helicopter guided by a pilot who is blind! It might be beautiful for a moment, but you'll miss much of the Grand Canyon and it's just a matter of time before you crash and burn!

> Some of these Old Testament roots are obvious and others are subtle.

And remember those two key words in Revelation 1:1? "Revelation" and "symbolize." That raised the question, What is the key for understanding the symbols that John used? We now have the answer: the Old Testament. John's readers would quickly make the connections with the Jewish Bible of their day, but the Romans wouldn't make those same connections. Revelation 1:1 could be paraphrased as "the unveiling of Jesus through the symbols of the Old Testament!"

Some of these Old Testament roots are obvious and others are subtle. Some are specific and others are general. Some of these have already been mentioned.

In the previous chapter we already noted that Revelation 1:13-16 sounds very similar to Daniel 10:5-6. And Revelation 1:4 presents "him who was, and is, and is to come" and that took us back to Exodus 3:14 where the great "I AM" appeared to Moses. And while Revelation also presents the seven Spirits, we noted that Isaiah 11:2 describes seven spirits. Let's be clear that these are not quotations. If fact, if you didn't know the Old Testament, you probably wouldn't even know that the inspired messages in Revelation have their roots in the inspired messages from the Old Testament!

Revelation 13:13 describes a beast coming out of the land, a beast who does great wonders and can even make fire come down from heaven in the sight of men. Can you think of any time in the Old Testament when that same kind of thing happened—people being wowed by fire coming down from heaven in the sight of men? The story that thrills children and adults alike, the story of Elijah with the Israelites and prophets of Baal on the Mount Carmel showdown is the Old Testament root (1 Kings 18:36-39) for this verse in Revelation 13:13. But note that in Revelation the fire falls on the wrong altar! Before projecting into the future and making guesses or assertions about what might happen in the future, one should first look back to the Old Testament. With that foundation the reader will have a better understanding of what John wrote in the book of Revelation.

Sometimes there is simply a general reference to something familiar in the Old Testament. In Revelation 1:12-13 John reports seeing seven candlesticks and one like the Son of Man walking among the candlesticks. Can you think of any Old Testament roots for candlesticks? Candlesticks serve an obvious function of light, but when you think of seven candlesticks or a seven-branched candlestick, the Old Testament root of the sanctuary comes to mind. Descriptions of these can be found in Exodus 25:31 and 2 Chronicles 4:7. In the New Testament light symbolized Jesus (John 8:12) and also his followers (Matthew 5:14). In case we didn't catch it in Revelation 1, John makes it doubly evident by having Jesus walking among the candlesticks, which he says are now the seven churches (Revelation 1:20).

The longest phrase in Revelation with an Old Testament root can be found in Revelation 14:7, "Worship him who made heaven and earth, the sea and the fountains of waters." Remember, there are no exact quotations from the Old Testament in the book of Revelation. John didn't want to come right out and name his

> Instead of looking at magazine cover stories, start with the Old Testament.

code book. But can you think of what Old Testament root John drew from for that long phrase, "Worship him who made heaven and earth, the sea and the fountains of waters"? The creation story of Genesis 1-2 contains this, but the wording actually matches more closely to the fourth commandment, found in Exodus 20:8-11. So when a person gets to Revelation 14:7, instead of looking forward, it's best to first of all look back to the Old Testament roots. With that understanding from what God has done in the past, a Bible reader obtains a better idea of what to look for in the present and the future.

In chapter two of this booklet we used the rider on the white horse in Revelation 6:2 to illustrate the four different schools of interpretation for the book of Revelation. Instead of looking to the first century, or the course of history, or some future rider, or even a personal application, what would happen if a Bible reader first looked to a possible Old Testament root. Could the reader find a rider on a white horse in the Old Testament? Actually, Revelation 6:1-8 has four horsemen on four colored horses—white, red, black, and pale. In Zechariah six, Bible readers would find four chariots pulled by four different colored horses. Surprise, surprise—they are the same colors that John used in Revelation six!

Sometimes the Old Testament roots make the meaning obvious. At other times these roots are helpful, but maybe not obvious. And at other times the similarity could be unmistakable, but the meaning might still be obscure.

You already knew that the book of Revelation has some connections with the Old Testament book of Daniel. But there are also plenty of Old Testament roots in books like Ezekiel, Zechariah, Isaiah, Jeremiah, Joshua, Deuteronomy, 2 Chronicles, Leviticus, Hosea, Exodus, Joel, 1 Kings, and even Song of Solomon! So key number five is to check for Old Testament roots. Instead of looking at magazine cover stories to understand the book of Revelation, start with the Old Testament.

Chapter 8

Key #6: Jesus Changes Everything

The story has been told about a pastor who was giving the children's story during the church service one day. He asked the kids, "What is small, has a bushy tail, scampers about on all fours, climbs trees, and stores nuts for the winter?"

The children scratched their heads and looked confused.

The pastor, feeling a bit desperate, tried again. "I know you know the answer to this, kids. Think about it. What animal is small, has a bushy tail, darts around on the ground, can be seen climbing trees, it collects nuts and stores them to eat later?"

Silence. Finally, little Tommy raised his hand slowly and only partway, but that was all the pastor needed. "Yes, Tommy. What am I describing?"

Tommy spoke tentatively, "It sounds a lot like a squirrel." Then Tommy announced triumphantly, "But I know the answer is JESUS!"

Why did Tommy think the answer was Jesus? Because that's the most common answer for a question pastors tend to ask children during the children's story.

This might be cute for children, but when it comes to both the Old Testament and the New Testament, the answer pretty much comes down to the same thing—JESUS!

The Old Testament finds its fulfillment in Jesus Christ and the New Testament grows out of Jesus Christ. Neither Testament makes sense without a focus on Jesus. And you can't understand the two together without Jesus connecting them. This requires a little more of an explanation and some examples to illustrate it.

Adam – Notice the description of Jesus at the beginning of the message to the Laodicean Church. According to Revelation 3:14, "To the angel of the church in Laodicea write: These are the words of the Amen, the faithful and true witness, the ruler of God's creation." That last phrase, "the ruler of God's creation" links the last book of the Bible with the first book of the Bible. Who would be the ruler of God's creation?

Check the Old Testament root by going back to Genesis 1:26, "Then God said, 'Let us make human beings in our image, in our likeness, so that they may rule over the fish in the sea and the birds in the sky, over the livestock and all the wild animals, and over all the creatures that move along the ground.'" The ruler of God's creation at the beginning was the human beings made in God's image—Adam and Eve.

In case you didn't catch it, you'll find the same thing in Psalm 8:5-6 (NIV) in the context of praise to God for what He created. "You made him [man] a little lower than the heavenly beings and crowned him with glory and honor. You made him ruler over the works of your hands; you put everything under his feet." God placed as the ruler over all creation the crowning work of His creation—humans!

While humans are still somewhat in this role, they lost most of it at the Fall when Adam and Eve chose Satan over God. They gave up their position as the rulers of Creation. Satan took their place. That's why John's naming of Christ as the ruler of God's creation (the Greek word is *arche*) alerts us to the fact that Jesus is the new Adam. Paul wrote a similar message in Romans 5:12-21. The ruler of Creation started as Adam and Eve, then they traded it to Satan, but Christ has become the "new Adam" and has rescued this planet from Satan. The Old Testament's ruler of Creation points forward to Jesus.

Moses – The great leader of God's people in Old Testament times, the one who took them from the slavery of Egypt through the wilderness and to the Promised Land, was Moses. According to Deuteronomy 18:15 (NIV), Moses told the people, "The Lord your God will raise up for you a prophet like me from among your own brothers. You must listen to him." While this can refer to God's messages to future generations through prophets in their own day, it finds its ultimate fulfillment in the Messiah—the object of all the Old Testament prophets.

Peter quoted this verse in reference to Jesus (see Acts 3:21). John the Baptist said he wasn't "the prophet" (see John 1:21). Philip referred to Jesus as the one Moses had predicted (see John 1:45). Jesus himself claimed that Moses had written about Him (see John 5:46). The people thought Jesus was this Prophet after he miraculously provided food to the masses (see John 6:14 and 7:40). And Moses even came to be with Jesus on the Mount of Transfiguration (see Luke 9:30-31). The great leader of God's people, Moses, points towards Jesus.

Aaron – While Moses led the Israelites from Egypt to the Promised Land, his brother, Aaron, functioned in the role of the high priest for the Israelites. The book of Leviticus provides specific details for setting aside both a place – the tabernacle that was God's visible presence among the people; and a people – the priests and Levites who mediated between the people and God. In essence, the priests connected the unholy people to the holy God by performing the rituals pointing toward forgiveness, purification, and reconciliation.

Repeatedly the death of a sacrificial animal represented that God would one day provide a sacrifice for all sins. Leviticus 16 describes the annual Day of Atonement in which Aaron, the high priest, served as the mediator for the entire assembly of God's people. The Old Testament priests and the role they performed pointed towards Jesus, our High Priest. Hebrews 7-8 describes how the priesthood of Jesus supersedes that of Aaron. Aaron, the great mediator as the high priest of God's people, points towards Jesus who is our High Priest.

Joshua – his name means "Yahweh is salvation" in Hebrew. The Greek version is "Jesus." Matthew 1:21 presents the angel's instruction to Joseph to name the Messiah "Jesus" because he will save his people from their sins. The Old Testament Joshua led God's people into the Promised Land and gave them rest (Joshua 1:13-15; 23:1). Jesus provides rest (Matthew 11:28) and additional rest beyond what Joshua could do (Hebrews 4:8-9).

Just as Joshua conducted the conquest of Israel's enemies (Joshua 6-12) Jesus conducted the conquest of Israel's enemies (Colossians 2:15) with victory over the principalities and powers. And as Joshua renewed the covenant with Israel at the end of his life (Joshua 24:14-15), Jesus renewed the covenant with his disciples at the end of his life (John 14-17; Luke 22:14-20). Jesus is the new Joshua.

> Jesus provides rest beyond what Joshua could do.

David – Without question, the quintessential king of Israel was King David. As a child he freed them from the giant bully, Goliath. As an adult, he led the nation to victory over all enemies. He paved the way for his son to construct the magnificent temple for God. The Jews expected their anticipated and promised Messiah to rule the nations as King David had. Sometimes they referred to the coming Messiah as the "Son of David." When Jesus asked the Pharisees whose son the Messiah would be, they replied, "The son of David." (Matthew 22:42) That led Jesus to quote Psalm 110:1 in which David stated, "The LORD (Yahweh) said to my lord (master), sit at my right hand until I put your enemies under your feet." The rhetorical question is how could King David have a lord/master? The answer: The "Son of David" known as the Messiah, is greater than King David.

When Jesus cleansed a demoniac, the people asked, "Could this be the Son of David?" (Matthew 12:23) When Jesus rode triumphantly into Jerusalem on the donkey shortly before his crucifixion, everyone knew that he was accepting the title of the Great

King. That's why people put palm branches and their coats on the road and shouted, "Hosanna to the Son of David!" (see Matthew 21:1-11.) King David pointed to the Great King to come.

Children of Israel – God called Abraham to start a nation that would be the conduit for God to bless the entire world. That line of people became known as the children of Israel. (Jacob's name was changed to Israel after he wrestled all night with God—Genesis 32:22-28.) The promises throughout the Old Testament continue to call for the Israelites to be God's people. But repeatedly they failed, even going into exile.

When one reads the Gospel of Matthew, written especially for the Jews (New Testament Jews are a continuation of the Old Testament children of Israel), a number of Old Testament quotations seemed ripped out of context to apply to Jesus. For example, Matthew 1:1 says that Jesus was the son of David and the son of Abraham. These figures represent God's people. Matthew 2:5-6 quotes Micah 5:2, naming Bethlehem as the origin of "The shepherd of my people Israel." Matthew 2:15 quotes Hosea 11:1, "Out of Egypt I have called my Son," which sounds much more like the children of Israel than Jesus.

And that is the point. The children of Israel find their true fulfillment in Jesus. When Herod murdered the babies in Bethlehem, the description brings up a quotation from Jeremiah 31:15 about "Rachel weeping for her children." A look at Jeremiah 31 provides a context of the promise to return from exile and to be God's people once again. That doesn't seem to fit the massacre Herod invoked. It's as though Matthew is taking the descriptions of the children of Israel and inserting Jesus as the new object or fulfillment of God's people. In the words of Jesus, "I didn't come to abolish the Law or the Prophets (the Old Testament) but to fulfill them." (Matthew 5:17)

Figure 2 shows that the Old Testament finds its focus and fulfillment in Jesus.

Jesus changes everything. That's key number six for finding Jesus in the book of Revelation. The Old Testament focuses on Jesus. That's exactly what Jesus explained to the two on the road to Emmaus after his

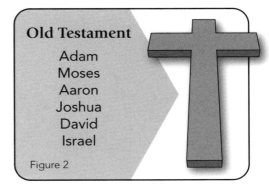

Old Testament

Adam
Moses
Aaron
Joshua
David
Israel

Figure 2

resurrection, "Beginning with Moses and all the Prophets, he explained to them what was said in all the Scriptures concerning himself" (Luke 24:27). Paul wrote that many read the Old Testament with a veil over their eyes, but that veil is taken away when Christ is the focal point of the Old Testament (see 2 Corinthians 3:14-16). Those who still can't see it would do well to read the New Testament book of Hebrews. In it, Jesus gets presented as "better" and "so much more" than the Hebrew elements of significance, such as angels, Moses, high priest Aaron, sacrifices, etc. Jesus himself said in John 5:39-40: "You search the Scriptures because you think that in them you have eternal life; it is these that testify about Me; and you are unwilling to come to Me so that you may have life."

Just as everything in the Old Testament finds its focus in Jesus, everything in the New Testament flows from Jesus. When the Bible centers on Jesus, what was *literal* in the Old Testament becomes *symbolic* in the New Testament. What was *local* in the Old Testament becomes *global* in the New Testament. Did you catch that? What was *literal* becomes *symbolic*; what was *local* becomes *global*.

Here are some examples. In the Old Testament, the literal children of Abraham were God's people. In the New Testament, God's people are the spiritual children of Abraham—those who place their faith in Jesus. According to Galatians 3:26-29 (NIV), "You are all sons of God through faith in Christ Jesus. For all of you who were baptized into Christ have clothed yourselves with Christ. There is neither Jew nor Greek, slave nor free, male nor female, for you are all one in Christ Jesus. If you belong to Christ, then you are Abraham's seed, and heirs according to the promise." Abraham's seed in the New Testament is the Church. Abraham's seed has gone from *literal* descendants of Abraham in the Old Testament to *spiritual* descendants of Abraham in the New Testament. Jesus changes everything!

According to Revelation 1:5-6, "Jesus loves us and has freed us from our sins by his blood, and he has made us to be a kingdom and priests to serve his God and Father—to him be glory and power for ever and ever! Amen." Before proclaiming the 10 commandments on Sinai to the Israelites, God told them they would be a "kingdom of priests and a holy nation." (Exodus 19:6) That didn't last long. Soon, Aaron and his sons were appointed to the role of priests, mediating between God and people. But God has always wanted direct access. And because of Jesus, we are now a kingdom of priests! The *literal* priests in the Old Testament tabernacle are transformed by Jesus so we are *spiritual* priests today with direct access to God! Jesus changes everything! Note figure 3.

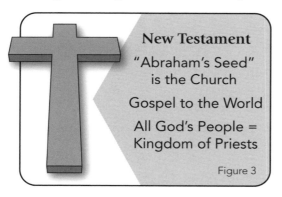

New Testament

"Abraham's Seed"
is the Church

Gospel to the World

All God's People =
Kingdom of Priests

Figure 3

Some Christians expect the literal people of Israel to be the fulfillment of the book of Revelation. But a focus on literal Israel today would take Jesus out of the center of our understanding and would deny that Jesus changes everything! This was very difficult for the Jewish Christians in the early Church to accept— that because of Jesus, Gentiles could instantly become part of the Church (see Acts 10-11 and Acts 15). A current focus on *literal* Israel today instead of *symbolic* Israel diminishes all that Jesus has done and continues to do.

Here's another example of the *literal* becoming *symbolic* because of Jesus. We no longer offer a literal lamb on an altar for the forgiveness of our sins. Jesus is the "Lamb of God, who takes away the sin of the world" (John 1:29). When we ask forgiveness for our sins, we don't take a lamb to church and slaughter it on the altar. We pray and our words of confession draw on the sacrifice Christ gave on Calvary.

We can apply this *literal* to *symbolic* change to something sensational in the book of Revelation, like the number 666. Sometimes called "the mark of the beast," located in a person's forehead or on the hand (Revelation 13:18; 14:9), a literal interpretation would look for a tattoo of the number 666 on a person's literal forehead or on that person's literal hand. But Jesus changes everything so what was literal in Old Testament times becomes symbolic in New Testament times. The number 666 becomes a symbolic number of ungodliness in a person's mind (forehead) or actions (hand).

Jesus changes everything! What was *literal* in the Old Testament becomes *symbolic* in the New Testament. But that's not all. What was local in the Old Testament becomes global in the New Testament. The Gospel Commission, Christ's parting words to his disciples following his resurrection, states, "All authority in heaven and on earth has been given to me. Therefore go and make disciples of all nations…" (Matthew 28:19-20) The book of Acts records it as, "You will be my witnesses in Jerusalem, and in all Judea and Samaria, and to the ends of the earth." (Acts 1:8)

Palestine, or "the Holy Land" becomes the entire world. What was *local* becomes *global*. Babylon is not some small country in the Middle East but every false system that wars against God or stands in contrast to God. That might include *your* country! Jerusalem is not a city occupied currently by Jews and Muslims. That is thinking *local*. When you see Jerusalem from a *global* perspective, Jerusalem includes all of God's people throughout the world.

Those infamous beasts in Revelation are not *literal* beasts, nor are they *local* beasts. They are *symbolic* and *global*. That will be important to remember when studying that portion of the book of Revelation!

Key number six for interpreting the book of Revelation is: Jesus changes everything! Note Figure 4. If Jesus isn't in the center, then we will miss the real focus of the Old Testament and we will lose the flow of the New Testament. With Jesus in the center, and recognizing that Jesus changes everything, we are better equipped to find Jesus in the book of Revelation!

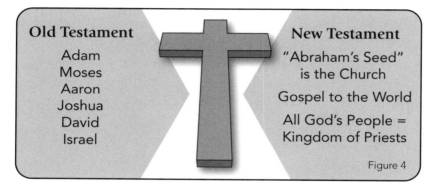

Old Testament

Adam
Moses
Aaron
Joshua
David
Israel

New Testament

"Abraham's Seed" is the Church

Gospel to the World

All God's People = Kingdom of Priests

Figure 4

Chapter 9

Key #7: Structure of the Book

Your English professor in college would probably view key number seven for interpreting the book of Revelation as the most obvious key of them all. From the standpoint of literature, most can quickly notice that the book of Revelation would get classified into the symbolic genre. But there are elements within the actual structure of the book that are instrumental for understanding the message. This might not be as exhilarating as connecting a current event to an obscure portion of the book, but it can provide consistent insights into the actual meaning of the book.

Parallels

One structural element that most can easily spot is the parallels throughout the book. Perhaps the most obvious would be the sets of seven. There are seven churches, then seven seals, followed by seven trumpets, and even seven plagues.

Some have noticed striking parallels when they compare the seven trumpets with the seven plagues. See Figure 5. For example, the sixth element in both of these includes special mention of the great river Euphrates, the primary river associated with Babylon. The parallels aren't as great or as striking when comparing the seven seals with the seven trumpets, although several are still

Parallel 7s

7 Trumpets Revelation 8:2 – 11:18		7 Bowls/Plagues Revelation 15:5 – 18:24
1/3 of Earth burned (Rev. 8:7)	1	Bowl poured on the Earth (16:2)
1/3 of Sea turns to blood (Rev. 8:8-9)	2	Sea turns to blood (Rev. 16:3)
1/3 of rivers & springs turn bitter (8:10-11)	3	Rivers and springs turn to blood (16:4)
1/3 of sun, moon and stars (8:12)	4	Sun (16:10-11)
Darkness from the Abyss (9:1-2)	5	Darkness on the beast's throne (16:10)
The Great River Euphrates (9:14)	6	The Great River Euphrates (16:12)
Loud voices in heaven; "Christ will reign forever" (11:15)	7	Loud voice from the temple throne; "It is done" (16:17)

Figure 5

Parallels between the 7 Seals and the 7 Trumpets

7 Seals	7 Trumpets
1 White horse	
2 Red horse	1 Fire and blood / 2 Fire and blood
3 Black horse, famine	3 Lack of water / 4 Darkness
4 Pale horse, death	5 Destroyer
5 Voices at the alter Incomplete # of the saved	6 Voice at the alter Incomlete # of the murdered
6 The day of wrath has come	7 Your wrath has come
7 Silence in Heaven	

Figure 6

noticeable. See Figure 6. For example, the third seal mentions a black horse and famine; the third trumpet mentions lack of water and the fourth trumpet tells of darkness. The fifth seal talks about voices at the altar, but it's the sixth trumpet that mentions a voice at the altar.

Recognizing the repetition and parallels helps us to anticipate some repeating of time periods rather than expecting a straight line of time—one set of seven following another set of seven. Just because the seven trumpets come *after* the seven seals in the book of Revelation doesn't necessarily mean the trumpets happen *after* the seals. The parallels lead us to consider that they might happen *at the same time,* but one set could give different input about *the same time* period.

Some other sets of seven might not be as obvious. The brief mention of the seven spirits before the throne (Revelation 1:4) gives a quick presentation of the number seven. Revelation also has seven beatitudes—blessings promised. See Figure 7. The first

The 7 Beatitudes/Blessings in Revelation

1 Revelation 1:3 – "**Blessed** is the one who reads aloud the words of this prophecy, and blessed are those who hear it and take to heart what is written in it, because the time is near."

2 Revelation 14:13 – "Then I heard a voice from heaven say, 'Write: **Blessed** are the dead who die in the Lord from now on.' 'Yes,' says the Spirit, 'for they will rest from their labor, for their deeds will follow them.'"

3 Revelation 16:15 – "'Look, I come like a thief! **Blessed** are those who stay awake and keep their clothes on, so that they may not go naked and be shamefully exposed.'"

4 Revelation 19:9 – "Then the angel said to me, 'Write: "**Blessed** are those who are invited to the wedding supper of the Lamb!"' And he added, 'These are the true words of God.'"

5 Revelation 20:6 – "**Blessed** and holy are those who have part in the first resurrection. The second death has no power over them, but they will be priests of God and of Christ and will reign with him for a thousand years."

6 Revelation 22:7 – "'Look, I am coming soon! **Blessed** are those who keep the words of this prophecy in this scroll.'"

7 Revelation 22:14 – "'**Blessed** are those who wash their robes, that they may have the right to the tree of life and may go through the gates into the city.'"

Figure 7

is found in Revelation 1:3, "Blessed is the one who reads the words of this prophecy, and blessed are those who hear it and take to heart what is written in it, because the time is near." The remaining six beatitudes all come in the second half of the book, which is also telling. There are also seven "woes" in the book of Revelation. And there are seven sanctuary scenes, which will be identified later in this chapter.

The number seven seems to be significant. Although only seven churches are mentioned, more than that existed in Asia when John wrote the book. Evidently the angel who communicated to John was intentional about using the number seven.

At times, the structure of the book of Revelation will be merely interesting. At other times, it will unlock the code that the symbols would hide if we didn't consider the structure of the book.

Numbers

The number seven seems to be quite significant in the book of Revelation. Are there any other numbers that come to mind when you think of this book? The sensational number 666 comes to mind quickly for some. Others focus on the 144,000. The New Jerusalem frequently uses the number 12—gates, foundations, measurements, etc. The throne room has four living creatures and 24 elders. There are four horsemen in Revelation six. There are three angels in Revelation 14.

> John's readers would first think of the *qualities* of a number.

But you won't find the number 13 mentioned in the book of Revelation. What is the significance of the number 13? Today we might consider the number 13 to be unlucky or an omen of bad things. It's one of the few numbers that has symbolic meaning to us, aside from individual preferences or premonitions like Michael Jordan's number 23 basketball jersey.

But that's today. Let's not forget that Revelation was written towards the end of the first century AD by a Christian with a Jewish background. He was relying on symbols from the Old Testament and his own current Jewish understanding. For the Jews, numbers are highly symbolic! For us, numbers first of all make us think of *quantities*. But for John, numbers would first make him think of *qualities*. When we hear about seven churches and seven seals, we think of the *quantity* of the number. But John's readers would first of all think of the *qualities* that the number seven represented. In fact there are several key numbers for the Jews and the early Christians. We don't often think in this vein, but we can discover what these numbers meant to them, which can increase our understanding of the book of Revelation.

The study of numbers is called *numerology*. Each letter in the Hebrew alphabet corresponded with a number. The same was true with Greek. A person's name had its own meaning, but it also had a number. For example, the name David means beloved. Taking the symbolic meaning of the letters adds up to 14 (d=4; v=6; d=4). In the Matthew 1 genealogy of Jesus, there are 14 generations from Abraham to David, 14 from David to the exile, and 14 from the exile to Jesus. Here's the numeric hint: Jesus is the new David!

In English we don't have that, so we usually think of numbers in terms of *quantity* rather than *quality*. But we can keep this simple. Let's start with just two primary numbers for Jewish thought when Revelation was written.

The first number is three. As Christians, when we think of the number three, it's easy to think of the Trinity—God. And that makes sense. But what about to the Jewish author? Three symbolizes holiness, which would be God as well. The presence of God for the Hebrews came in the wilderness tabernacle. The dimensions of the Most Holy Place, in cubits, was 10 x 10 x 10, or 10 three times—a cube. The number three also shows up in terms of the three parts of the tabernacle: the courtyard, the Holy Place, and the Most Holy Place. Inside the Holy Place were three pieces of furniture: the candlestick, the table of showbread, and the altar of incense. Even the Old Testament Scriptures can be thought of in three portions: the Law, the Prophets, and the Writings (Psalms, Proverbs, etc.). In the book of Revelation, the heavenly sanctuary description in chapter four has creatures saying day and night, "Holy, holy, holy is the Lord God Almighty, who was, and is, and is to come." (Revelation 4:8) Did you catch the 3s before and after "the Lord God Almighty"? The three before are "holy, holy, holy." The three after are "who was, and is, and is to come." Three symbolizes God.

> 3 + 4 means adding God to this world.

The second number is four. This represents the earth. Think of the four major points on a compass, or the four corners of the earth (Revelation 7:1; Isaiah 11:12) or the four horses of Revelation (6:1-8). The three angels' messages of Revelation 14 include proclaiming the everlasting Gospel to those who dwell on the earth. That group gets reiterated with four terms—every nation, kindred, tongue and people. Why the repetition? Because the four synonyms emphasize the symbol or quality of the number four—the earth. The everlasting Gospel is for the entire earth!

So we have two primary numbers: three represents God and four represents the earth.

Notice what happens when adding God and the earth together, that is, when we add three plus four. Three plus four equals seven. First grade arithmetic covers that *quantity*. But the *quality* of three plus four goes much deeper because of the symbolism. The number seven shows up repeatedly in Revelation. Symbolically, adding three and four together means adding God to this world. When we do that, we have perfection—the number seven! That's the Gospel! The number seven is considered the perfect number or the symbol of completeness. That matches Paul's message to the Colossians, "In Christ dwells all of the fullness of the Godhead bodily, and you are complete in Him. (Colossians 2:9-10,

NKJV) Of course, three plus four equals seven—God brings the world to perfection. By the way, the number six indicates falling short of perfection or completion. Six is the number of man. Consider the Creation story. On what day was man created? And then in Revelation, that tantalizing number 666 is called the number of a man (Revelation 13:18).

Notice happens when multiplying God and the earth: three times four. The *quantity* is the number 12, but the *quality* or the symbolic meaning of that number would provide a different meaning. In Old Testament times one would automatically associate the number 12 with the 12 tribes of Israel. In New Testament times one would automatically think of the 12 apostles. But what about in the book of Revelation itself? Twelve is the kingdom number. Notice how the New Jerusalem gets described in Revelation 21 and 22. It has 12 gates with 12 angels at the gates. On the gates are written the names of the 12 tribes of Israel. You'll find 12 foundations with the names of the 12 apostles. The measurements of the city are 12,000 stadia by 12,000 stadia, by 12,000 stadia. Wait, isn't that the shape of a cube? 12,000 three times. And this is where God dwells! It must be the Most Holy Place!

Depending on which translation of the Bible you have, the dimensions of the city might lose their symbolic meaning. This happens when the English translators think of numbers in terms of *quantities* rather than *qualities*. They think John is trying to be precise in the actual size of the city rather than comprehending that the symbolic book of Revelation uses numbers as part of the symbolism. The King James Version calls it 12,000 furlongs (Revelation 21:16). Same with the New King James Version. The New International Version calls it 12,000 stadia, as does the New Century Version. But the New American Standard Bible and the Contemporary English Version list it as 1,500 miles. The New Living Translation says it was 1,400 miles and then gives a footnote of 12,000 stadia in Greek, which is 2,200 kilometers. Oops! You just lost the symbolic meaning! In order to keep the numbers as *qualities* rather than merely *quantities*, note whether or not the Bible you use maintains the numbers as symbols rather than transposing them into literal quantities such as miles or kilometers.

Elsewhere in Revelation, one can read about the inhabitants of the city who are referred to as the 144,000. Some math wizards quickly notice the kingdom number of 12 in that: 12 x 12 x 1000 = 144,000. Some people spend a lot of time and a lot of energy debating whether the number 144,000 is literal or symbolic. Here's a hint: It's in the book of Revelation! Here's another hint: Numbers in Revelation primarily refer to *qualities* rather than *quantities*.

What about the number 10? This can symbolize completeness, as in counting the 10 fingers and 10 toes on a newborn. In Old Testament terms, the number 10 brings to mind the 10 commandments—the short version of God's law that get a longer description in the first five books of the Bible (sometimes referred to as "the Law"). So 10 could be the minimum needed for completion. The number 10 can also refer to enduring hardship or difficulty, like when Daniel, Shadrach, Meshach and Abednego were tested 10 days. There were 10 plagues in Egypt. The Feast of Trumpets lasted for 10 days and led to the Day of Atonement or Day of Judgment.

Related to the number 10 is the number 1,000. Some would factor it into 10x10x10, which is 10 multiplied by itself three times. Symbolically this could mean God's completion or God's testing. The number 1,000 could also be used to describe a tribe or a military battalion. You might recall that after the boy David killed Goliath, the women of Israel sang out, "Saul has slain his thousands, and David his ten thousands" (1 Samuel 18:7). We might think that Samuel didn't know his math because Saul hadn't killed anyone and David killed only one person! But we would be missing the symbolic meaning of the numbers. King Saul's army took out the Philistine battalion, but little David completely outdid him! Today when we exaggerate, we might say, "David was 100 times better than Saul." The Hebrews would say 10 times better—completely better. And that's how Daniel and his three friends performed compared to the rest after three years of training in Babylon. They were 10 times better than all the wise men in the kingdom (Daniel 1:20).

Not surprisingly, some people really get caught up in numerology. The important thing for us to remember is that when Revelation mentions numbers, first of all consider their *qualities* before considering their *quantities*. For a quick summary, consider Figure 8.

What Does that NUMBER Mean?

Numbers in the book of Revelation are typically symbolic, which means they represent qualities rather than quantities. Sometimes the numbers are blatant, and other times they are subtle.

3 – God, Holiness

4 – Earth

7 (3+4) – Perfection

6 – Man

12 (3x4) – Kingdom

10 – Complete, Testing

1,000 (10x10x10) – Military unit, God's complete testing

24 (12+12) – Patriarchs (OT) and Apostles (NT)

144,000 (12x12x1,000) – All of God's people, ready for battle

Figure 8

Pyramid

One more important element when it comes to the structure of the book of Revelation is an overview of the book as a whole. When we read a book, we usually start at the beginning and read all the way through until the end. Sometimes we cheat and read the end early because we know that's the really good part—the climax to the story or presentation. The same is true when we watch a movie. The plot builds and builds until it climaxes at the end. And most of us like it when it comes out as some form of, "And they lived happily ever after." This is linear thinking.

But that is not the way people in the Middle East would have composed a story or poem or other forms of literature. They followed a completely different format that we could call a pyramid. They called it a chiasm, based on the Greek letter X (chi – pronounced "key"). They would match the beginning and end in some way. And along the way, there would be other elements that would match in corresponding ways. See Figure 9. It's easy to expect that the beginning and end could match. But other parts matched as well. This doesn't mean a word-for-word copy, but allusions and phrases and key words would show up in both places.

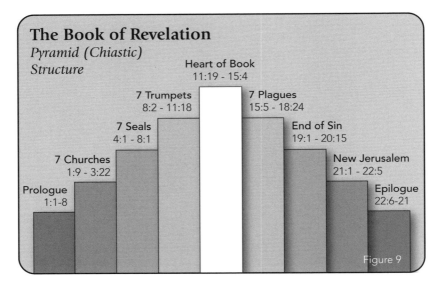

Let's look at a few examples from the perspective of an overview. Of course the prologue and epilogue share some similarities, but notice the way the seven trumpets and the seven plagues match up. Refer back to Figure 5 and Figure 6 on page 54. The trumpets start with thirds of destruction on the earth, then the sea, and then the rivers and springs. The plagues follow the same pattern, but it's no longer thirds. The plagues must be more intense than the trumpets. There are other similarities as well. This can be helpful when elements on one side of the pyramid aren't easy to decipher. Comparing them to what's matching or what's similar on the other side might provide a helpful clue for one's understanding.

But the most significant thing of the pyramid structure is what comes in the middle—at the peak of the pyramid. The most important part of the book gets placed in the middle, not at the end. And that's not the way we're accustomed to thinking in the Western world. The book of Revelation ends with God's people joining Him in heaven. Isn't that the climax? It's certainly one type of climax. Those who say, "I read the end of the book and God wins," are right, but that's not the primary message of the book of Revelation. The most important message from John would be put in the middle of the book, at the peak of the pyramid or chiasm.

If we knew where the different sections of Revelation started and ended, that would help us tremendously in knowing how to study it in its sections. The chapters and verses we follow today weren't put into the Bible until the 1500s, well after the book of Revelation was written. They make a handy reference tool to locate specific parts, but they weren't necessarily placed in the most ideal spots for dividing up the book. If only there was some clue, maybe something that John would have used to let his readers know that it was time for a transition. What could he use in his code?

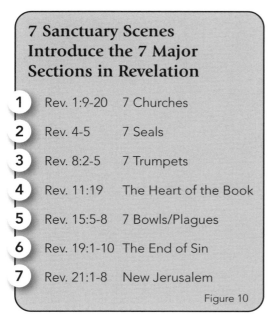

7 Sanctuary Scenes Introduce the 7 Major Sections in Revelation

1	Rev. 1:9-20	7 Churches
2	Rev. 4-5	7 Seals
3	Rev. 8:2-5	7 Trumpets
4	Rev. 11:19	The Heart of the Book
5	Rev. 15:5-8	7 Bowls/Plagues
6	Rev. 19:1-10	The End of Sin
7	Rev. 21:1-8	New Jerusalem

Figure 10

With the book being the Revelation of Jesus Christ, some have found that the sanctuary scenes in the book mark the divisions John intended for his readers. Would you be surprised to find seven sanctuary scenes in the book? See Figure 10. Each of these sanctuary scenes not only sets off another section of the book of Revelation, but it gives a clue to understand that section. Those who knew about the Jewish sanctuary components and services would be able to make that link. Some of the descriptions are lengthy and some are very short. But the introductory sanctuary scenes should be considered with the section of the book they initiate.

The pyramid structure of Revelation places the study of this book into a whole new light. Reading it the way it was written gives insight that Western readers in the 21st century wouldn't see initially. Looking at numbers for their symbolic qualities rather than their literal quantities adds meaning and clarity. Parallels and repetition make the student of Revelation more aware of themes and time periods. Considering the structure of the book of Revelation might seem technical, but it can transform the study of Revelation from individual creativity to a powerful message from God.

Chapter 10

Taking the Next Step

You have seven keys for finding Jesus in the book of Revelation. Are you ready to jump into the book? Go for it! Utilize these seven keys:

Key #1 – The literary context. What comes before and what comes after the portion being studied?

Key #2 – The historical/cultural context. Put yourself into John's day to understand the book before making applications today.

Key #3 – Key words. Look for key words that contain key portions of the message. Compare how those words are used in other places in Revelation and the Bible as a whole.

Key #4 – Compare with the rest of Scripture. This can be done with key words or key themes or descriptions.

Key #5 – Look for Old Testament roots. Where are Revelation's symbols used in the Old Testament? Look back to connect the symbol to its roots rather than projecting forward to some unknown future.

Key #6 – Jesus transforms everything. Jesus is the center of the whole Bible. The Old Testament points to Him and the New Testament grows out of Him. What was literal becomes symbolic; what was local becomes global.

Key #7 – The structure of the book. Look for repetition and parallels, like the sets of sevens. Consider numbers first for their symbolic quality rather than their literal quantity. The pyramid structure clarifies the flow of the book, its symmetry and high point.

As we studied the book of Revelation with fresh eyes and using these seven keys, several things happened. First of all, we found ourselves overwhelmed with how amazing, awesome, and magnificent Jesus is. Indeed, it proved to be a revelation of Jesus Christ to us! Secondly, some of the specific details we thought we knew, well, we're not so sure about some of these any longer. And we're okay with that. Thirdly, the broad themes now seem so obvious to us that we wonder how we got so sidetracked on the details and missed the bigger picture.

> We found overselves overwhelmed by Jesus.

What are those major themes in the bigger picture? From beginning to end, we've noticed that God desires to be in a covenant relationship with his people—"I will be their God and they will be my people." Jesus is Lord of heaven and earth, although the earth continues to be a battlefield until sin and death get destroyed by Jesus. Satan has been exposed as a supernatural being who uses coercive power and deception, even teaming with political and religious entities to create a false trinity. Another theme is God's long suffering mercy that continues to reach out to save. Repentance doesn't seem like a popular topic these days, but its necessity seems to be a recurring theme in Revelation. Evil and sin often seem to be in the driver's seat and even appear to win, but Satan really does lose, and he loses everything. God's people need deep trust in God and enduring patience since God's timing doesn't always match our timing.

For those who get stuck or confused and want additional outside help, we recommend the primary sources that we found most helpful in our study. Go to your book source (such as www. amazon.com) and search for books by Jon Paulien, Ranko Stefanovic or Jacques Doukhan. We gratefully and happily endorse those resources.

This booklet, *Seven Keys for Finding Jesus in the Book of Revelation*, presents the guidelines we followed in the Revelation 101 seminar we conducted for the Carmichael Seventh-day Adventist Church. We have revised those presentations and put them in a format for others to use as well.

Of course readers can find much more to Revelation than what we covered in our 10 sessions. We named it "Revelation 101" to indicate a beginning class for college freshmen. If you're capable of thinking like a college freshman, you should be able to follow this series. We hope that pastors and small group bible study leaders will find this to be a helpful tool as they seek to lead others (as well as themselves) to discover a revelation of Jesus Christ through the symbols of the book of Revelation.

As this booklet went to press, the rest of the Revelation 101 sessions were being reviewed by scholars, pastors, administrations, educators, and small group leaders. Once that feedback has been received, final edits will be made and the materials will be made available. Perhaps you will want to obtain them to lead a group to study Revelation in your church or home or school or place of work. The materials will be available to order online at www. Revelation101.com.

The collection of materials will be in a 3-ring notebook for the leader and a *Participant's Guide* for the participants. The *Leader's Manual* includes the following seven components:

1. Verbatim of the 10 sessions – A word-for-word presentation of each session. A person could literally read the entire seminar/bible study out loud to a group, or read it for how it could be presented and then adapt it to one's own use. This provides the entire presentation for each session with tips for the presenter.

2. Outline of the 10 sessions – In contrast to the verbatim of each session, the outline is a shorter version that simply presents the main points. This is more efficient and flexible for leaders who personalize the material.

3. Very brief outline of the 10 sessions – Just the bare essential points are found in the short, 1-page "brief outline."

4. Deeper study materials for the 10 sessions – For the presenter who wants or needs more information, the deeper study materials provide additional substance for more research or to respond to questions that may come up along the way. These correspond to the same topics presented in the outline and verbatims, and follow the seven keys for each session.

5. PowerPoint slides – Simple slides that can be projected to direct participants to specific portions of their *Participant's Guide* or to illustrate a portion of the presentation. No special effects or transitions have been included so the slides illustrate the material rather than dominate the presentation. These are also available in Keynote for Mac users.

All of this comes in hard copy and electronic format.

6. *Participant's Guide* for all 10 sessions – A complete booklet for each participant allows each one to follow along, add personal notes and markings to aid in understanding and to take for future reference. Additional copies of these can be obtained so participants can personalize their own copy.

7. Electronic format for editing in addition to hard copy of everything already listed – All of this comes in hard copy and also in electronic format (Microsoft Word documents and PowerPoint files [Keynote for Mac]). This enables the presenter to edit, adapt, cut-and-paste, and personalize each presentation.

The 10 sessions cover the following segments of the book of Revelation. The first two sessions present the seven keys for finding Jesus in the book of Revelation. This matches what you've read in this booklet. The remaining sessions deal with one segment of the book, as identified in the pyramid structure of the book. Because the center of the pyramid marks the heart and the most important part of the book, two sessions have been allocated to that segment of Revelation. The 10 sessions cover the following topics:

Session 1 – Introduction; First four keys for interpretation
Session 2 – Three more keys for interpreting Revelation
Session 3 – The Seven Churches
Session 4 – The Seven Seals; the 144,000 and great multitude
Session 5 – The Seven Trumpets; the scroll; the two witnesses
Session 6 – The False Trinity: Dragon, Sea Beast, Land Beast
Session 7 – The Three Angels; the Two Harvests
Session 8 – The Seven Bowls/Plagues
Session 9 – Final Blessings and Curses
Session 10 – Face-to-Face with Jesus; Summary and Conclusion

To purchase the *Leader's Manual* and also bulk orders of the *Participant's Guide*, go to www.Revelation101.com.

As this booklet ends, consider a few personal questions.

Do you want a revelation of Jesus Christ—more than what you have seen, known, or experienced before?

That certainly describes what has happened to us! When we looked at the text itself and considered the historical/cultural context before applying it to our day and place, we saw more of Jesus and less of our own ideas. When we looked at key words like "revelation" and "signify/symbolize" we discovered entirely new insights from a host of Old Testament roots. This startled us and demonstrated how consistent God has been throughout history and how Jesus is central to the entire Bible. Instead of triggering our excitable imaginations to free-form any type of explanation that zipped through our heads, we learned to de-code the symbols by looking at their Old Testament roots.

Is the book of Revelation God's message for you? Of course it has been God's message for others, but what about for you?

We found ourselves wowed by what we discovered about this incredible God. We now trust Him even more in areas that are still unknown.

Are you willing to take a similar journey? If you are, we believe the book of Revelation will indeed be a revelation of Jesus Christ to you.

Notes

Chapter 1
[1] Some of their publications include from Jon Paulien: *Revelation: Hope, Meaning and Purpose,* 2010; *Seven Keys: Unlocking the Secrets of Revelation,* 2009; *What the Bible Says About the End Time,* 1998; and a 5-set; 12 CD series verbal commentary, 2004. From Ranko Stefanovic: *Revelation of Jesus Christ,* revised 2009. From Jacques Doukhan: *Secrets of Revelation: The Apocalypse Through Hebrew Eyes,* 2002.

[2] Such as Hans LaRondelle, Kenneth Strand, William Shea, Mervyn Maxwell, Roy Naden, and Edwin Thiele.

Chapter 2
[1] A helpful comparison of the four schools of interpretation in parallel format can be seen in Steve Gregg's *Revelation Four Views* published by Thomas Nelson Publishers in 1997. This commentary includes a variety of interpretations for each school, but the same themes consistently get repeated.

[2] All Scripture passages are taken from Today's New International Version (TNIV) unless noted otherwise.

Chapter 3
[1] Paulien, Jon. *Seven Keys: Unlocking the Secrets of Revelation.* Pacific Press. Nampa, ID. 2009. Page 97.

Scripture References